Rewire Your Stress Reaction:

Strategies to Transform Focus and Activate Your Resilience

Cynthia Howard RN, CNC, PhD

Performance Expert.
Executive Coach

Copyright © 2019 Cynthia Howard RN, CNC, PhD

ISBN: 9780692865897

Cover design by Todd Siatkowsky, Special Forces Art Department

Printed in the United States of America

The Work SMART Club is a subsidiary of Ei Leadership · www.eileadership.org

Change the way you think and you will change your life.

Dr. Cynthia Howard

Table of Contents

Welcome to the Course 6

    Resources and Contact Information: 6

About the Author 7

The Stress Effect 8

    FAST TRACK TRIGGERS 11

What Are Your Goals for this Course? 15

Long Term Impact of Stress 16

    NOTES 17

Energy leaks 18

    Depletion grid 18

    Resilience Toolkit (Energy Management) 19

Resilience: #1 Skill You Have Never Been Taught 26

    NOTES 27

The Resilience Pyramid 28

    Resilience Roadmap Assessment 29

        How to Plot Your Scores 34

        Plot Your Scores from The Resilience Assessment 35

        What Your Scores Mean 36

        3 Things 39

        The Resilience Roadmap in practice... 40

        Journal 41

3 Levels of Managing Stress: 42

    NOTES 43

Stress Strategies 44

    Stress SWOT 44

        Your Stress SWOT 45

    Visualization (Mindset) 46

        Step 2: Energy Clearing Step of Visualization 50

        Tips to Make Visualization Work for You 54

        A Simple Exercise in Visualization 55

FAQ: Frequently Asked Questions About Visualization 56

Everyday Gratitude & Appreciation (Mood).. 57

Grati-Slips 61

Journal... 62

Re-Frame: Beyond the BS around Stress – Your Belief System!........................ 64

Overview.. 66

Blank ABC Chart.. 67

NOTES 68

Introduction to Mindfulness.. 69

Setting Up Your Daily Practice.. 71

Action Plan.. 72

Journal... 73

NOTES 74

Work SMART Club 80

WELCOME TO THE COURSE

Hello, I look forward to going through this life changing program with you. I have worked with thousands of professionals, hundreds of leaders and have seen tremendous transformation when using these tools. Here is what one of my leaders had to say, after taking this course:

> *"I did not want to quit my job. I knew I could make a difference and did not want to give up. When I started to have physical symptoms from the pressure, my choices seemed like they were black or white – stay at the job and keep suffering or quit- and risk shortchanging my potential. I didn't have any tools to deal with the stress. This course has been powerful. It has given me a new perspective and the skills to deal with the pressure of home, family and work."*

Rewire Your Stress Reaction offers a way out from the negative consequences of stress; backed by decades of research and used by millions of people all around the world. You are on your way to renewal.

This workbook is part of the online program that has video, audio and additional resources. As you go through the online videos and the exercises, post your questions and comments in the private Facebook group. This group offers a network where you can learn and grow.

Resources and Contact Information:

1. Be sure to request access to the Facebook Group. This is your support group, place to ask questions, experience live training and discussions.

2. Stop by "Office Hours" (dates/ times posted in the Facebook group) and talk about your specific issues. Feel free to post any questions in the Facebook group; use the #questions.

3. If you have technical issues, contact support@eileadership.org.

4. If you would like to schedule a complimentary consultation to discuss 1:1 coaching, please visit www.worksmart.club/strategy-session.

5. Stay subscribed to our emails. They guide you through the course, provide great tips, include challenges and special offers!

ABOUT THE AUTHOR

Cynthia Howard RN, CNC, PHD

Pioneer of the Resilient Mindset.
Performance Expert.
Fellow, AIS (American Institute of Stress)
Green Belt Lean Sigma
Certified Scrum Master

Licensed
Heartmath Trainer
& Provider

In a 20 + year coaching practice, Dr. Howard has worked with leaders, business owners, professionals, helping them move beyond the barriers that limit progress. With a background as a Registered Nurse and graduate degrees in psychology, Cynthia researched what makes individuals successful and what gets in the way of progress.

Working with thousands of people, Cynthia developed the 5 Levels of Resilience Pyramid, organized around mindset, energy management and the science of performance. She recognizes that stress is the threat to fulfilling potential and loving life.

Author:

The Resilient Leader Mindset Makeover: Let's Uncover the Elephant in the Room

Everyday Emotional Intelligence: A Guide to better Communication. Learn to Handle Fatal Emotions, Drama, Conflict and Bullying.

Rewire Your Stress Reaction. Change the Way You Think: 4 Step C.A.R.E. Method

H.E.A.L: Healthy Emotions. Abundant Life.

THE STRESS EFFECT

Stress is part of everyday life. In this module we help you understand how stress impacts you physically. Chronic unchecked stress contributes to premature aging and illness.

Watch the short video online; it illustrates what is happening in your body when stressed.

The stress reaction is a primitive survival instinct. We are hardwired to react to real and imagined events which is why living in the age of Distraction a source of constant triggers. This is why we want to help you FOCUS and strengthen your emotional awareness; this will help you reduce the frequency of stressful reactions.

We will be sharing proven tools help you transform your stress reaction and prevent the negative consequences of unchecked stress. But first, it is important to understand what is happening in your body; even though you cannot see the impact of stress, doesn't mean it is not serious.

Has stress hijacked your best?

Stress is hard to define because we all experience it somewhat differently. I have heard some say, "life is stress!" Others are energized by challenges and thrive on the rush that comes from the pressure.

A 'technical' definition of stress: *the condition experienced when the demands, at work or personally, exceed the capacity an individual has available to them.*

Let's start with understanding how stress affects you. Take the self-assessment.

The following represents ways that stress can show up for individuals. Check all that apply. This can help you tune into yourself and what happens when you experience stress.

Physical Reaction to Stress

Symptom	Frequency Daily Weekly Monthly	Severity 1 Minimum 10 Severe	Symptom	Frequency Daily Weekly Monthly	Severity 1 Minimum 10 Severe
Headaches			Sweating		
Joint Pain			Rapid Heart Rate		
Heartburn			Colds, Flu		
Indigestion			Sinus Trouble		
Fatigue			Irregular Heart Rate		
Constipation			Forgetfulness		
Neck Pain			Concentration Difficulty		

If you checked three or more boxes, there are lifestyle changes needed to avoid more serious health challenges. Chronic, unchecked stress contributes to premature aging. You will have the opportunity to set up a self-care program to address these and other signs of chronic stress.

Denying the experience of stress only increases the negative consequences. Everyone has their own capacity for stress and this changes at different times in life. This self-assessment will build on your self-awareness and ultimately your self-management.

Now, let's look at the next step: Emotional and Spiritual Signs of Stress.

Emotional/Spiritual Signs of Stress

Symptoms	Frequency Daily Weekly Monthly	Severity 1 Minimum 10 Maximum	Symptoms	Frequency Daily Weekly Monthly	Severity 1 Minimum 10 Maximum
Tension			Worry		
Irritability			Loss of Motivation		
Depression			Cynical/Sarcastic		
Anger			Weight Gain		
Rage			Food Cravings		
Call Out Sick			Can't Fall Asleep		
Can't Stay Asleep			Racing Thoughts		
Negative			Pessimistic		
Want to Run Away			Isolates from Friends		
Never Enough Time			Could Jump Out of My Skin		
Addicted to Facebook			Increased Alcohol Use		
Wake Up Tired Even After 8 Hours Sleep			Work Shifts and Rotates Days and Night Shift		

FAST TRACK TRIGGERS

I really do not know what got into me. I called the pharmacy to find out where the medication was that the doctor had just ordered, and they said it was on its way. When my coworker said she was going to lunch, I lost it. I was caught off guard and suddenly felt angry. I had worked so hard all morning and expected her to understand what I needed. I was so busy that I had not told her what I needed. Realistically, she can't read my mind. Wow, I went from calm to crazy in seconds!

Can you think of a time when you found yourself reacting to something, only later to realize you were over the top? Is there a pattern?

Write down 3 things you react to at work:

1.
2.
3.

Write down 3 things you react to at home:

1.
2.
3.

Give examples of your "stressed" self-talk:

_____

_____

_____

Do you spend time re-hashing old conversations or interactions? Write out an example.

_____

_____

What <u>could</u> you be doing with this time?

What Happens in Your Body When You Feel Stressed? (Stress hijacking)

With over 86 billion neurons and the processing power that surpasses the best super computer, why is it hard, at times, to say what you want to say, how you want to say it?

This flight, fight or freeze reaction triggers the emotional parts of the brain (limbic system). The cortex or thinking part of the brain is the largest and the last to respond, unless you have activated your resilience and learned to respond under pressure.

When triggered, first you feel, and then you think.

The cortex is where the higher functions of the brain operate. Your 'executive function' in the brain where decisions are made, and judgement is exercised short circuits under chronic pressure and the stress reaction.

Hardwiring:

Primitive Brain

Emotions

Thinking

So then what? Let's look at an emotional hijacking next... Remember the stress reaction is a primitive survival instinct. Think of this as the operating system for your nervous system; it has not been upgraded in 100,000 years!

Emotional Hijacking: Fast-Track Stress Reaction

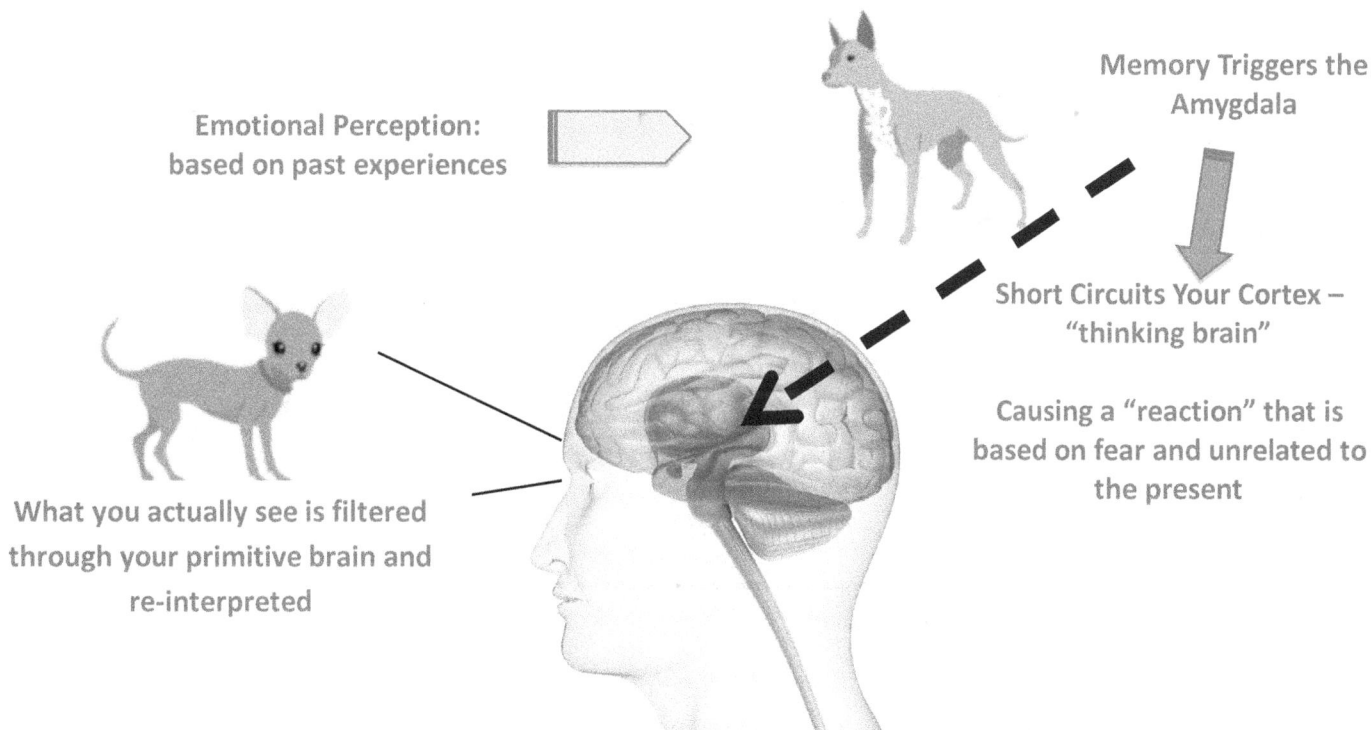

Emotional Perception:
based on past experiences

Memory Triggers the
Amygdala

Short Circuits Your Cortex –
"thinking brain"

Causing a "reaction" that is
based on fear and unrelated to
the present

What you actually see is filtered
through your primitive brain and
re-interpreted

The "Fast-Track" is when the stressor triggers the survival instinct and your logical, analytic, rational part of the brain becomes unavailable. Your thinking cortex's ability to decide about the stressor is overridden by the *primitive,* fast-track process of the amygdala. We all have these filters from the past through which all new experiences are perceived. The greater your capacity for stress (resilience), the less reactive you are.

You are hard wired for survival and the amygdala will react immediately bypassing your thinking brain. The link from the amygdala to the cortex alerting you to danger is much stronger and more well-developed than from your thinking brain to the amygdala. ***This means that your stress reaction is going to be stronger and faster than your thought to stop it.*** In this program, we help you reset your stress point, giving you more control over this reaction.

Most of the reactions people have at work, as well as in personal relationships, are a result of this trigger.

The tools we provide will strengthen your ability to respond rather than react.

Rust out: Boredom

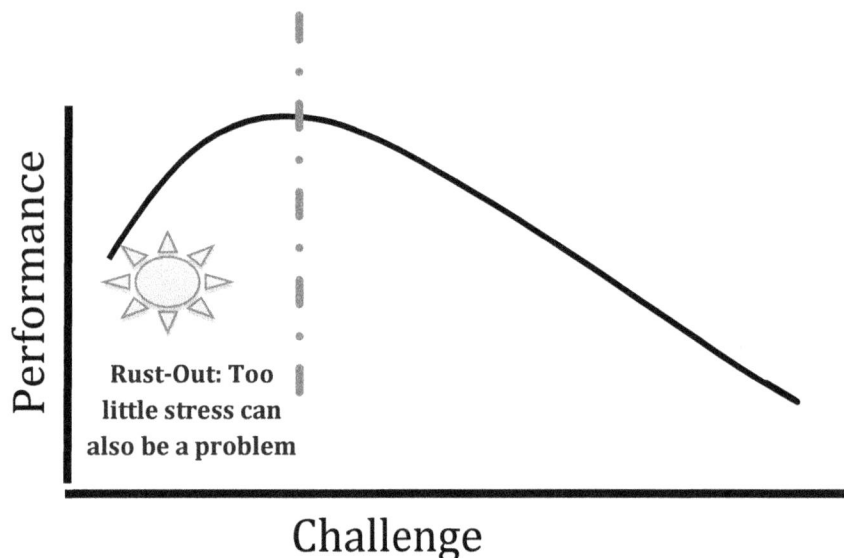

Performance (y-axis) vs Challenge (x-axis)

Rust-Out: Too little stress can also be a problem

Are you living in your comfort zone?

Rust-out is the opposite of burnout. This is when there is not enough stimulation to keep you engaged and can happen when you are working below your capacity level.

Do you have periods of rust-out? Explain:

_____

_____

_____

_____

_____

If you struggle with boredom, answer the questions on the online module.

WHAT ARE YOUR GOALS FOR THIS COURSE?

To make this process more meaningful, set up a goal for yourself. What do you want to see differently as a result of this program?

_____

_____

_____

_____

Another way to look at this is to identify how chronic stress, overload, reactivity is interfering with accomplishing your desired outcomes. What could your day look like without it:

_____

_____

_____

_____

Having a clear idea of what you want to see happen, _differently,_ in your day/ life/role will help you achieve it!

LONG TERM IMPACT OF STRESS

Are you aware of how stress affects you? The first module provided you with a look at how stress impacts you physically, mentally and even spiritually.

This module will help you tune into how everyday stress accumulates and skews your ability to cope. This intensifies the negative consequences of the stress reaction.

Visit the online portal and download the stress log. This will help you track the day to day triggers. This helps you set up a plan to buffer yourself against the stress. Keep the log for one week and jot down how everyday experiences impact you. Instructions are included on the document.

Cumulative Stress: Schedule of Recent Events

Download this schedule, online, and follow the instructions. As you go through each type of event, you will be scored on the degree of long-term stress.

What did you learn?

_____

_____

_____

3 Ways Stress Impacts You:

- Mood
- Energy
- Mindset

We will be going into what happens in the body and mind later in this course. We also provide strategies that help you address all three areas.

NOTES

ENERGY LEAKS

View the video on Energy leaks. What came to mind for you about your own day and areas where you lose energy? Are there recurring negative and defeating thoughts?

_____

_____

_____

_____

_____

_____

Depletion grid

Grab your copy of the Depletion Grid and go through the exercise described in the video. The Depletion to Renewal Exercise is helpful to uncover energy drains and emotional patterns. Keep a grid with you to use on the go.

Use the Resilience Toolkit to quickly boost your energy and unhook from the energy drains.

The Resilience toolkit is presented next.

Resilience Toolkit (Energy Management)

I have found the tools in this section, when practiced minutes a day, quickly activate one's resilience. Resilience is more than "bouncing back."

Think of resilience as your capacity.

Capacity is how much of something you have. Just like your smart phone, when you have a fully charged battery, you can use all the apps and maximize the use of your phone.

What is it like when your capacity is low? What do you notice?

_____

_____

What could you accomplish with more energy and focus? Identify one thing you want to achieve but fall short due to lack of energy.

_____

_____

_____

_____

The Science of Performance

Be sure to watch the 20-minute video, online, and learn why these tools are so powerful!

The tools on the next several pages are from Heartmath's toolkit of "Intelligent Energy Management." … enjoy them!

The following tools and techniques are from the Institute of Heartmath and come with registered trademarks. HeartMath is a registered trademark of the Institute of HeartMath. emWave®, Heart Focused Breathing®, Heart Lock In®, Quick Coherence are registered trademarks of Quantum Intech, Inc (dba HeartMath, Inc.). Inner-Ease™ is a registered trademark of Doc Childre, one of the founders of Heartmath.

Go to the online membership and watch the videos on these tools... The instructions are repeated here in your Course Guide.

Heart Focused Breathing®

Focus your attention on the area of your heart. Imagine your breath is flowing in and out of your chest area; breathing a little slower and deeper than usual.

Suggestion: Inhale 5 seconds, exhale 5 seconds, (or whatever rhythm is comfortable.)

This is the first step in your coherence building tools. It helps you unhook from the stress reaction and the distracting emotions that may have been triggered. This ability to pause, gives you greater flexibility in how you will respond.

Why do we focus our attention on the area of the heart? Research shows that where we focus our attention, physical changes occur in that area. By shifting attention to the heart area, you will shift your heart rhythms into a more coherent state.

Practice using this tool throughout the day. All of these tools have a cumulative effect; the more you use them, the greater impact they will have. And the longer they will have that impact. We have video on the membership site that talks about the research and the impact of these tools. Be sure to visit the site and watch these videos. It will help you understand what a significant difference these tools can make in your life.

Think of something you do frequently during the day. Are you walking down hallways, going to the printer, to a certain department? Practice this technique during that time. Start to associate that activity with Heart Focused Breathing®. It will help you build a new habit!

Check off those times you will commit to using Heart Focused Breathing for 60-90 seconds:

- ❑ Before you get out of bed
- ❑ While getting ready for work
- ❑ Before your staff meeting
- ❑ Before you walk in the door at home

Are there other times that are ideal for you to begin this habit?

Quick Coherence®

Step 1: Engage Heart Focused Breathing®. Focus your attention on the area of your heart. Imagine your breath is flowing in and out of your chest area, breathing a little slower and deeper than usual.

Suggestion: Inhale 5 seconds, exhale 5 seconds, (or whatever rhythm is comfortable.)

Step 2: Make a sincere attempt to bring up regenerative feelings like appreciation, gratitude, love.

Suggestion: Try to re-experience the feeling you have for someone you love, a pet, a special, an accomplishment, etc., or focus on a feeling of calm or ease.

Coherence is an optimal state when mind, emotions and body are in sync. During the stress reaction, the body is using up precious fuel to handle the depleting emotions and the physical strain on the body. Renewing emotions create coherence. It is coherence that restores the body and renews the spirit. Be sure to watch the video on the membership site to better understand what is happening in the body and why coherence is so significant.

When would you use this tool?

Be sure to practice this when you do not need it! Then use this anytime you want to unhook from a draining emotion, to reset your baseline, unhook from a difficult conversation. As with all the tools, use them with your eyes open and you will find you can use them more often. And no one has to know what you are doing!

Freeze Frame®

Step 1: Acknowledge the problem or issue and any attitudes or feelings about it.

Step 2: Heart focused breathing®.

Step 3: Make a sincere attempt to experience a regenerative feeling such as appreciation or care for someone or something in your life.

Step 4: From this more objective place, ask yourself what would be a more efficient or effective attitude, action or solution?

Step 5: Quietly observe any subtle changes in perceptions, attitudes or feelings. **Commit to sustaining beneficial attitude shifts** and acting on new insights.

Freeze Frame® is a multipurpose technique to help you shift perspective, plug energy drains, improve clarity, and find innovative solutions to problems or issues.

This technique combines the tools you have learned so far, helping you increase your coherence. Coherence enhances mental functions (thinking & decision making) and helps you tap into a wider range of intelligence.

It can be used when you are feeling stressed to "freeze the frame" and avoid a knee jerk reaction. Most people find that using the Freeze Frame Technique, they have greater insight and increase their awareness.

If you are not able to make the shift and come up with a new solution to your challenge, do not worry! This technique can take practice. Keep using it. You may get the insight or new approach days later.

Use the following worksheet and write out your process.

Identify the challenge you want to shift:

_____

_____

_____

_____

After using Freeze Frame, what insights came through from this process?

_____

_____

_____

_____

_____

How would you describe the problem now, having gone through this process?

_____

_____

_____

_____

_____

Heart Lock in®

Step 1: Heart Focused Breathing

Step 2: Activate and sustain a regenerative feeling such as appreciation, care or compassion.

Step 3: Radiate that renewing feeling to yourself and others.

Start using this technique in 1-minute increments and gradually increase to 3, 5, 15 minutes, and longer. This practice is powerful. Use this anytime you must wait for something. It can be your secret!

Consider taking the 15 in 15 Day Challenge. Doing 15 minutes of Heart Lock in per day for 15 days. You can break this up into 3- or 5-minute increments if you like.

The Heart Lock in® can be used at the start of your day, before a business meeting, before tough conversations, any time you want to feel in sync, clear and focused.

Use this when:

- ❑ You are struggling with someone and are not sure how to resolve the dilemma.

- ❑ You are worried about your family, child, partner.

- ❑ You want to reduce wear and tear from unchecked stress from the chaos of the day.

- ❑ Any time you want to build a coherent field with teams, families and communities.

When will you use the Heart Lock in? What do you notice after using it?

_____

_____

_____

_____

_____

_____

The Heart Lock in® Challenge

Will You Take the Challenge?

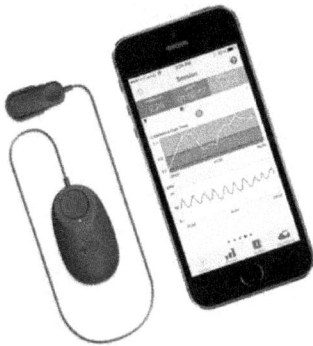

15 minutes of Heart Lock in in 15 Days

Share in the Facebook Group!

You can do this in one 15-minute increment at the start of your day (ideal) or in three 5-minute increments, prior to each meal. Or any combination that works for you.

This will be a great way to fast track your "resilience bank account." What could you do with a fully charged battery?

How will you use the Heart Lock in? Share in the facebook group!

RESILIENCE: #1 SKILL YOU HAVE NEVER BEEN TAUGHT

The stress reaction interrupts the ability to think clearly, make great decisions show up at your best. Unchecked pressure drains your energy and contributes to early burnout.

Did you know more than half of leaders' burnout in 18 months?

Below is a grid depicting the fine line between performance and pressure. Do you know when you cross the line?

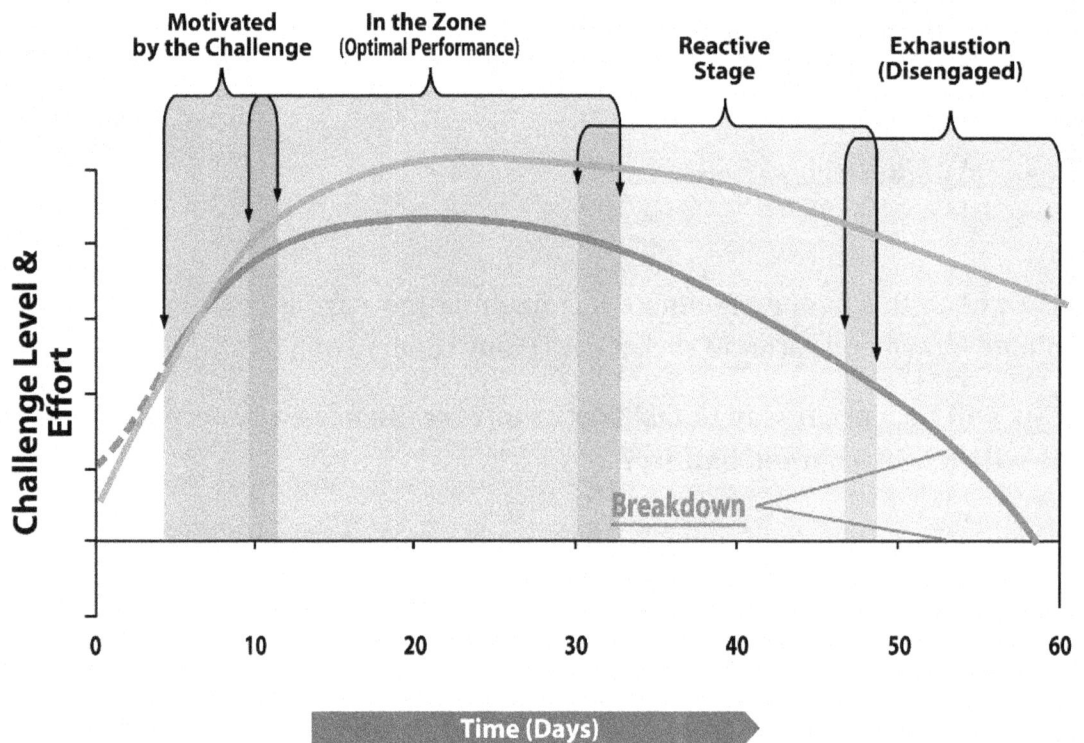

Watch the video online as Dr. Cynthia Howard describes this graph...

NOTES

THE RESILIENCE PYRAMID

Resilience is capacity.

Think of it as your inner battery. Your resilience depends on the choices you make every day and will vary depending on what is going on. This is to be expected. We cannot always control what is happening; we do have the ability to control how we respond. As you increase your awareness of how you respond under pressure and the choices you make as a result, you will strengthen your resilience (capacity).

The beauty of this system and the tools we incorporate, is you strengthen your resilience in just minutes a day; building your capacity over time. The simple daily practice of these tools increases self-awareness, the foundation of emotional intelligence and authenticity. You will continue to reap the benefits over time in just minutes a day.

These practices can literally add years to your life (the science proves it) and will add life to your day as you choose to shift out of a frantic, stressed out mode to one that is deliberate, joyful and in charge.

After working with thousands of individuals I recognized a pattern many people go through in coming back from burnout and stress overload; this pyramid was developed to illustrate this journey. It is natural to go back and forth between levels, this is not a linear process, but more like a spiral. The key is to increase your awareness at each level, master the basics and move to the next level.

Do the reflection exercises in this course; they will deepen your awareness. *Self-awareness is key, especially as it relates to your daily choices.*

Resilience Roadmap Assessment

This 5-dimension self-assessment helps you tune into each level of resilience. Evaluate yourself and answer based on the 1 (low) to 10 (high) scale. Think about your life, today, and rate your responses. Be honest. This is to help you gain insights into how you respond under pressure, what happens to your mindset when under pressure and if your daily choices support your goals. It is for your eyes only, so it pays to be objective.

To score each section, add up the numbers given to each question and divide by 10. You will plot your score on a map so you can quickly see what area needs your attention.

Energy Management

1. I exercise at least 20 minutes, 4 out of 7 days.   1 2 3 4 5 6 7 8 9 10

2. I eat vegetables and fruit daily; minimum of 3 servings.   1 2 3 4 5 6 7 8 9 10

3. I drink at least 8- 8oz glasses of water each day.   1 2 3 4 5 6 7 8 9 10

4. For every fast food meal eaten in a week, subtract a point from the total of 10. *(For example, if you have eaten 1 fast food meal, subtract 1 point; 5 meals in a week, 5 points.)*   1 2 3 4 5 6 7 8 9 10

5. I wake up feeling rested.   1 2 3 4 5 6 7 8 9 10

6. I drink coffee and or energy drinks to get going. Subtract a point for every drink to boost energy in the week.   1 2 3 4 5 6 7 8 9 10

7. I am satisfied with my weight.   1 2 3 4 5 6 7 8 9 10

8. I have maintained my weight in the last month.   1 2 3 4 5 6 7 8 9 10

9. I have all the energy I need to do what I have to do in the day.   1 2 3 4 5 6 7 8 9 10

10. I have the energy to be creative.   1 2 3 4 5 6 7 8 9 10

Add up the numbers for each question and divide by 10.

TOTAL   **DIVIDE =**

Notes:

Self Care (Stress Tolerance)

1. I spend time reflecting and tuning in to my feelings.   1 2 3 4 5 6 7 8 9 10

2. I receive as much as I give in my personal relationships.   1 2 3 4 5 6 7 8 9 10

3. I learn something new every month.   1 2 3 4 5 6 7 8 9 10

4. I can say no without feeling guilty.   1 2 3 4 5 6 7 8 9 10

5. I spend money on myself.   1 2 3 4 5 6 7 8 9 10

6. I tune into what I feel and support my needs throughout the day.   1 2 3 4 5 6 7 8 9 10

7. I have a list of "self-care" strategies and do something every day for myself.   1 2 3 4 5 6 7 8 9 10

8. I am aware of when I am stressed and need "me" time.   1 2 3 4 5 6 7 8 9 10

9. I easily communicate my needs to others and respect theirs.   1 2 3 4 5 6 7 8 9 10

10. I look at myself in the mirror and enjoy what I see.   1 2 3 4 5 6 7 8 9 10

Add up the numbers for each question and divide by 10.
TOTAL   **DIVIDE =**

Notes:

_____

_____

_____

_____

_____

Mindset

1. I have all the time I need in a day.	1 2 3 4 5 6 7 8 9 10
2. I see the glass half full.	1 2 3 4 5 6 7 8 9 10
3. I am in charge of my personal life.	1 2 3 4 5 6 7 8 9 10
4. I am in charge of my professional life.	1 2 3 4 5 6 7 8 9 10
5. I easily adapt to the daily challenges that show up.	1 2 3 4 5 6 7 8 9 10
6. I manage stress well.	1 2 3 4 5 6 7 8 9 10
7. I balance the demands in my day and also give myself time.	1 2 3 4 5 6 7 8 9 10
8. I bounce back from setbacks.	1 2 3 4 5 6 7 8 9 10
9. I acknowledge mistakes and/or failures and keep going.	1 2 3 4 5 6 7 8 9 10
10. I show up every day and do the best I can.	1 2 3 4 5 6 7 8 9 10

Add up the numbers for each question and divide by 10.

TOTAL _____ DIVIDE = _____

Notes:

_____

_____

_____

_____

_____

Influence (Relationships)

1. I make time to spend with my family. 1 2 3 4 5 6 7 8 9 10

2. I am happy with the amount of time spent with friends. 1 2 3 4 5 6 7 8 9 10

3. I make time for my partner every day. 1 2 3 4 5 6 7 8 9 10

4. I make time to talk with my children about what is happening in their lives. 1 2 3 4 5 6 7 8 9 10

5. I make the time to get to know my co-workers and/or my staff. 1 2 3 4 5 6 7 8 9 10

6. I like myself and am comfortable with who I am. 1 2 3 4 5 6 7 8 9 10

7. I am satisfied with my closest relationships. 1 2 3 4 5 6 7 8 9 10

8. I have fun in my personal relationships. 1 2 3 4 5 6 7 8 9 10

9. I am productive in my work relationships. 1 2 3 4 5 6 7 8 9 10

10. My relationships are balanced in give and take. 1 2 3 4 5 6 7 8 9 10

Add up the numbers for each question and divide by 10.

TOTAL   **DIVIDE =**

Notes:

_____

_____

_____

_____

_____

Flow

1. I engage in a daily spiritual practice with prayer, meditation and mindfulness.

1 2 3 4 5 6 7 8 9 10

2. I am guided by core values in my daily life.

1 2 3 4 5 6 7 8 9 10

3. I make choices based on my values.

1 2 3 4 5 6 7 8 9 10

4. I feel fulfilled.

1 2 3 4 5 6 7 8 9 10

5. I volunteer my time.

1 2 3 4 5 6 7 8 9 10

6. I support causes important to me with time or money.

1 2 3 4 5 6 7 8 9 10

7. I "unplug" every 4 hours for at least 15 minutes.

1 2 3 4 5 6 7 8 9 10

8. I enjoy quiet time in nature.

1 2 3 4 5 6 7 8 9 10

9. I spend time alone and reflect on my life and accomplishments.

1 2 3 4 5 6 7 8 9 10

10. I am inspired by the miracles that show up in my life.

1 2 3 4 5 6 7 8 9 10

Add up the numbers for each question and divide by 10.

TOTAL   DIVIDE =

Notes:

How to Plot Your Scores

Use this graph to plot your scores from each section. Take a highlighter and highlight the number associated with your score, in each of the five categories. (Round up if needed.) This gives you a quick visual to see what sections have low scores and may require more attention from you. Make a note in each column about what is working at this level of resilience.

EXAMPLE

	Energy	Self Care Awareness	Mindset	Influence	Flow
10					
9					
8					*I want to be more focused on my goals than absorbed in my problems.*
7					
6					
5		*Tuned in and aware of how stress impacts my body.*		*When I manage my interruptions, I am more available to my team.*	
4					
3	*Increased fast food. Not enough water.*		*Conflict increases my negativity.*		
2					
1					

Plot Your Scores from The Resilience Assessment

10					
9					
8					
7					
6					
5					
4					
3					
2					
1					
	Energy	**Self-Care Awareness**	**Mindset**	**Influence**	**Flow**

What Your Scores Mean

First, look at each section individually.

Energy Management

This level of the resilience pyramid is about your daily choices and how you manage your energy through, food, exercise, sleep, water; the basics of a healthy lifestyle.

If you scored:

<5 You are at risk for increased reaction to stressful events. Without the fuel your body needs to maintain your stamina, there is a tendency to use coffee, sugars, tobacco and other stimulants to keep going. This sets up a vicious cycle. You could be in a cycle of crash and burn or perpetual slow motion, not accomplishing what you would like to get done.

6-8 You are focused, *most of the time*, and able to make choices that support your energy needs. Look at your answers, where is the energy leak? Does it show up with diet, what you drink, your movement or lack of, or your sleep?

8.5+ Congratulations, you are able to maintain certain disciplines that work for you regarding daily lifestyle choices. It is important to have a plan to keep them up.

Stress Tolerance

The second level of the resilience pyramid has to do with your ability to manage your stress. This level is really about self-awareness. If you do not know how situations (and people) impact you, how can you change how you respond?

If you scored:

<5 You are not tuned into your preferences and your needs. This increases the risk of being hijacked by the stress reaction and being drained. This course will help you learn more about you and provide proven self-care practices you can use in just minutes a day.

6-8 You are learning more about your needs and making a conscious effort to take care of you. On what questions did you score the lowest? I hope you will share on the Coaching Calls, or in the Facebook group; we can offer you suggestions.

8.5+ Congratulations, you are managing your stress and aware of what you need. Be sure to set up a plan to keep it up.

Mindset

The third level of the resilience pyramid has to do with how you think. Do you maintain your perspective when under pressure? What you think, believe and feel drives your actions and your presence as a leader.

If you scored:

<5 You may be struggling with maintaining your perspective. Did you know you can learn to be optimistic?

6-8 You have success with forward perspective, *sometimes*, but may be caught by unchecked pressure. Read through the questions and jot down the circumstances in which you scored low. In this course, you will learn proven tools that will transform your stress reaction and increase your resilience. This is the first step to a resilient mindset and consistently maintaining it.

8.5+ Congratulations, you are staying resilient and your perspective is focused on possibility. Now set up a daily plan to keep your mindset resilient.

Influence

The fourth level of the resilience pyramid is focused on relationships. This is your ability to influence and your awareness of the importance of connections. Every level builds on the next one. As you consistently take care of you, being able to focus on others is natural and easier.

If you scored:

<5 Have you shut down and withdrawn due to increased pressure? You may be under reacting or withholding your emotions or have stopped sharing your feelings because of the increased pressure. This course offers you proven steps to unhook from the debilitating pressure of unchecked stress.

6-8 You have learned to balance results with relationships however still tend to sacrifice the opportunity to connect authentically with people at work or intimately with those closest to you. Stay tuned. In this course you will learn to increase your awareness and mindfulness, making your ability to authentically connect with others easier.

8.5+ Yay! You are staying connected with others at work and in your personal life. Now set up your plan to ensure you do not lose those connections.

Flow

The final level of the resilience pyramid is where you have mastered daily choices, managed your mindset, connected with others and now can go through your day in flow. This is the state of mind where you are focused on what is important and connected to the purpose behind the mission.

Flow is a state of mind that occurs naturally. Most people have had the experience of losing the sense of time when involved in an activity. As you learn to build your resilience you will be able to deliberately engage flow for greater satisfaction at work and in your close relationships.

If you scored:

<5 Are you super focused on getting it all done? Have you lost your curiosity or wonder at everyday miracles? Do you avoid spending time alone? Compulsive busyness is not a long-term strategy to get more done.

6-8 You are actively mindful and tuned into your values, making time to review and reflect. There still may be a tendency to solve other people's problems, losing touch with your own purpose and mission.

8.5+ You have learned to FOCUS while still maintaining relationships. You are enjoying challenges. What do you need to do more of, and less of, to consistently engage flow?

The Resilience Roadmap is a way to think about the full scope of resilience. It is not a destination, rather you will travel back and forth between the levels. Stay open and continue to learn more about what works for you and what does not. This system requires a few minutes of daily practice for a profound shift in mindset. This course will move you ahead and give you easy to use, proven tools, backed by science, so you can get more done without burning up or out.

Now, onto 3 Things...

3 Things

Having gone through the assessment, were you able to identify daily choices or behaviors that drain your energy? Or keep you from achieving your goals – consistently?

On this chart jot down 3 things you will do LESS of...

I also believe you have identified things you are doing now, that work well for you. As you eliminate the destructive choices and behaviors, what can you DO MORE of to *consistently* achieve your goals?

3 Things I will do to more of ...	3 Things I will do less of ...
1.	1.
2.	2.
3.	3.

Are you ready and willing to commit to these 3 things, daily?
Consistency is key.

Watch the video online about the 5 Levels of the Resilience Pyramid. We also have the downloadable file if you want to read about each level.

The Resilience Roadmap in practice...

This is a very quick and simple example of how you can engage the 5 levels in your day.

1. Imagine yourself starting the day by tuning into yourself and setting your intention. **(Influence)**

Just for today, I will not anger...

2. Drink a glass of water with fresh lemon vs coffee. Practice heart focused breathing for 3 minutes. **(Energize)**

3. Smile more at people you see on the street or in your office. **(Flow)**

4. Spend your lunch in a mindfulness state of mind as you eat. **(Self care)**

5. Regardless of the events, keep a positive attitude. **(Mindset)**

On the next page is a Journal prompt. How will you put the roadmap into practice? Keep it simple!

Journal

Reflect and write about what you learned taking the Resilience Assessment. What do you see or understand about your daily choices and behaviors as you go through your day?

How will you put the Resilience Roadmap into practice?

Energy management · Self Care (Awareness) · Mindset · Relationships (Influence) · Flow

3 LEVELS OF MANAGING STRESS:

Action:

When possible, take action to change some aspect of the situation. When this is not possible, focus on the other steps.

Awareness:

Is your perspective big enough to understand the situation? What emotions might be limiting your view?

Acceptance:

Sometimes, you need to accept that this is a trying situation and just get through it.

This module has a variety of strategies you can use to manage the stress reaction. We highly recommend you choose 2-3 strategies (including the ones in the Resilience Toolkit) and practice at least one per day for 2 weeks. At the end of two weeks practice another strategy every day for two weeks. Do this even when you are not feeling pressured. This ensures you will have the ability to use this tool when the feeling of stress shows up. It also helps to build in a discipline to manage your energy and awareness.

NOTES

STRESS STRATEGIES

Stress SWOT

You have probably done a SWOT analysis for your team. We are going to use this model to explore the internal and external stress triggers that may be impacting you.

The more aware you are of what and how you are impacted, the greater opportunity you must make adjustments. Use the "Schedule of Recent Events" to identify potential threats.

STRENGTHS

What are your strengths when it comes to handling/ managing stress?

Skills

Support networks, family, friends, colleagues

Resources: i.e., Flexible schedule, paid time off

WEAKNESSES

Read through the list and see what applies to you. These are areas that weaken your ability to manage your stress.

- Impulse control
- Lack of emotional awareness?
- No support network?
- Do you lack resources?
- Are you currently in a draining relationship, dealing with illness, your own or family, experiencing financial trouble?

OPPORTUNITIES

What opportunities exist for you right now? If you had more capacity what is available to you?

Think about possibilities in your industry/ field/ organization.

THREATS

What can un-checked stress cost you if you do nothing?

Are there threats in the environment that could cause greater pressure or challenge if not addressed?

There is a blank SWOT on the next page, fill it in based on what you have learned doing these self-assessments ...

Your Stress SWOT

STRENGTHS   **WEAKNESSES**

OPPORTUNITIES   **THREATS**

Visualization (Mindset)

Einstein not only changed the foundation of scientific thinking when he introduced the theory of relativity ($E=MC^2$), he changed the way people thought about the world. He acknowledged his genius was the result of using both his analytic brain and infusing it with the flow of creativity to help shape his theories and conclusions. Another of his quotes:

"Imagination is more important than knowledge."

Right before he wrote about the speed of light, he had a dream of riding on a moonbeam. There are other stories of imagination creating a breakthrough in conventional wisdom. Kekule, famous chemist and founder of the theory of chemical structure, discovered the structure of the benzene ring during a daydream when he saw an image of a snake eating its tail. He also saw dancing atoms and molecules and came up with the theory of chemical structure.

These discoveries changed the foundation of science and how people saw the world. They came from the integration of both the right and left sides of the brain; a blend of analytic and creative intelligence.

The fact is, our brain naturally thinks in images. This is how we all learned to speak, write and learn. Visualization is a power tool that integrates your natural instinct to think in images with the rational mind.

Origins of Imagineering

In 1940's Alcoa wanted to keep up the demand for their one product, aluminum. They created a program that blended imagination with engineering to come up with innovations. They called it, "Imagineering." Today that word is trademarked by Disney to reflect how they combine imagination with engineering to transform swampland into a remarkable theme park.

This blend of imagination and analysis is at the foundation of resilient thinking and the style of visualization I am introducing here. For over twenty years, I coached thousands of individuals to change the way they thought including breaking free of anxiety, self-doubt, fear and other destructive patterns of thinking and feeling. To break through the client's resistance and clarify their goal, I used techniques like hypnosis, imagery, and energy clearing to shift their attention and thought patterns. Working with so many people over the course of twenty years, I learned a lot about changing behavior (and mindset) to achieve success.

Your brain naturally thinks in images.

Everything we learn, our brain first 'sees' it as an image. We easily accessed this as a child; we were inclined to use our imagination in play as a natural instinct. During school years, this inclination was quickly extinguished in the process of learning. Most people did not notice the loss of this great skill until life threw them a curve ball and forced them into a major transition.

This is when most of my clients sought help, either their business, career or marriage was falling apart and they needed help making sense of it all. I want to share this tool to help you not just avoid hitting the wall, but to also increase your everyday innovation and creativity. Once you learn this, you can use it in any situation to discover new and effective ways to operate.

Resilient thinking is grounded in this power tool. I will first take you through the process of visualization and then walk you through your analysis. This two-step process of visualization is more effective in moving beyond the roadblocks of limiting beliefs or mental models that are outdated or too small.

When you deliberately use the power of visualization, you will increase your opportunity to succeed and achieve the very thing you want – even when it seems out of reach. You will expend less effort by using this approach by losing the worry, fear, or doubt about how things will turn out.

Worry and fear are the negative use of visualization. Stop working against yourself.

Visualization is the intentional use of your mind to achieve success.

How you use your attention determines your success. Visualization is the deliberate and intentional use of your attention. Use this process to experience the desired outcome before conversations with employees, your boss, or the Board. It is great to use as you plan for your new initiative and see all things working out the way you want them. Using visualization in this way helps you relax while you practice the situation in your mind, going through all the steps 'as if' you were actually doing it.

Golfers, musicians, and all successful people use this power tool to practice and develop skills and, in essence, increase confidence, muscle memory, and the results they want.

Chronic stress sets up a fear-based motivation, and you spend time imagining worst-case scenarios or engaging in negative, worrisome thoughts and catastrophic thinking. Knowing what we know about the plasticity of the brain, getting stuck in negative limited thoughts can quickly become your default perspective. Your brain adapts to the thoughts and activities you most often engage, and this becomes your default mode of thinking.

How do you direct your attention?

Are you focused on what isn't working and feeling gloomy?

Are you focused on possibility and feeling empowered?

It is your choice.

Tune into your thoughts. On what do you focus? Keep this log for 1 day. What did you discover?

Begin a practice of regular visualization of what you want (as opposed to worrying about what you fear might happen). You will be surprised to learn it increases your confidence. With a regular practice of visualization, you enhance skills and strengthen feelings of empowerment. You are also relaxing while you *experience the outcome you really want*. This changes your attitude, approach, and perception of what is happening as well as changing how you come across to others. Relaxed leaders are more creative and effective.

Visualization helps keep your motivation high. It is common and typical for motivation to wax and wane. In the beginning of a new program, motivation is strong and everything is easy. As the weeks move on, your desires may seem less as stress takes its toll on your enthusiasm. As challenges show up, your resolve may weaken.

You need a "motivation reboot." You have probably experienced this when you have started a new diet or exercise plan or when you decided to change a bad habit. This is also true for any new initiative at work. As the day-to-day tasks grind away at you, it is easy to get bogged down in the details; your goals for starting your new program may be further away in your mind and harder to get excited about.

Whenever you are rolling out a new program at work, keep the results you want in the forefront of your mind. Visualization helps you create a success map.

What do you want to have happen? What will your day or life look like as a result of this new program?

Define it, and then imagine it. Experience it, feel it, and get as detailed as possible. Hold the expectation. Really feel the achievement of this goal. Use this tool with all things big and small. Do you have trouble communicating with an employee? See your next conversation flowing smoothly. Do the same with your spouse, children, and friends. Release the struggle of trying too hard and use visualization to see what you want to happen.

Do you want new skills in communication, optimism, resilience, and emotional intelligence? See you interacting and succeeding. Just as with mindfulness, when your mind wanders and brings up questions, distracting thoughts, or problems, go back to the image of you handling the problems and seeing everything going your way. This is a good exercise in building confidence. This is a competitive edge you will have as you adopt this power tool.

As life demands more of you, it is easy to give your energy to the urgency right in front of you, leaving yourself frustrated and feeling negative about what is possible. A regular habit of visualization will keep you focused on your goals.

Researchers who criticize the use of visualization, citing a decrease in motivation as a result of seeing success, acknowledges the brain reacts "as if" the imagined scenario actually happened.

What the above research demonstrates is that even though visualization doesn't *always* motivate, it does change your brain. In other words, this process is powerful. Let's look at step two of my visualization process next.

Step 2: Energy Clearing Step of Visualization

This step will help clarify your goals and create very specific visualizations. You are going to do some analysis on your desired goals.

For the sake of this exercise, think of something you would like to accomplish through visualization. This does not have to be your biggest goal. Choose something you can use to work through this process.

Identify your goal in measurable terms:

i.e., I want to lose 15 lbs., wear a size 6, earn $250,000, or get promoted to Director of the department...

_____

_____

_____

_____

On the next page, think about WHY this is not possible for you. Jot down your answers. (Don't worry, we are going to clear these limiting beliefs)

Why not you? List at least 3 reasons you should not get this goal?

1.

2.

3.

[You will use energy clearing on this shortly. If you can list more than 3 reasons, put them down.]

Why not NOW? List 3 reasons why NOW is not the right time.

1.

2.

3.

[You will use energy clearing on this next. If you can list more than 3 reasons, put them down.]

You do not have to figure out your resistance. Write out how it shows up and any self-talk that accompanies it.

Energy Clearing: Step 2 of Visualization

As you read through the 2 lists on the other page, tap or rub on the 2 points. They are just below your clavicle and outside of your sternal notch.

Read through the list and tap or rub, allow whatever emotion to flow as it comes up, releasing it with every tap. Spend 5 minutes going through this process. It is important to keep tapping when you feel the emotions come up.

THIS IS A RELEASE EXERCISE. If you stop tapping when emotions come up – you shut down the release process.

I have a video demonstration of the full technique of Tapping in the online program.

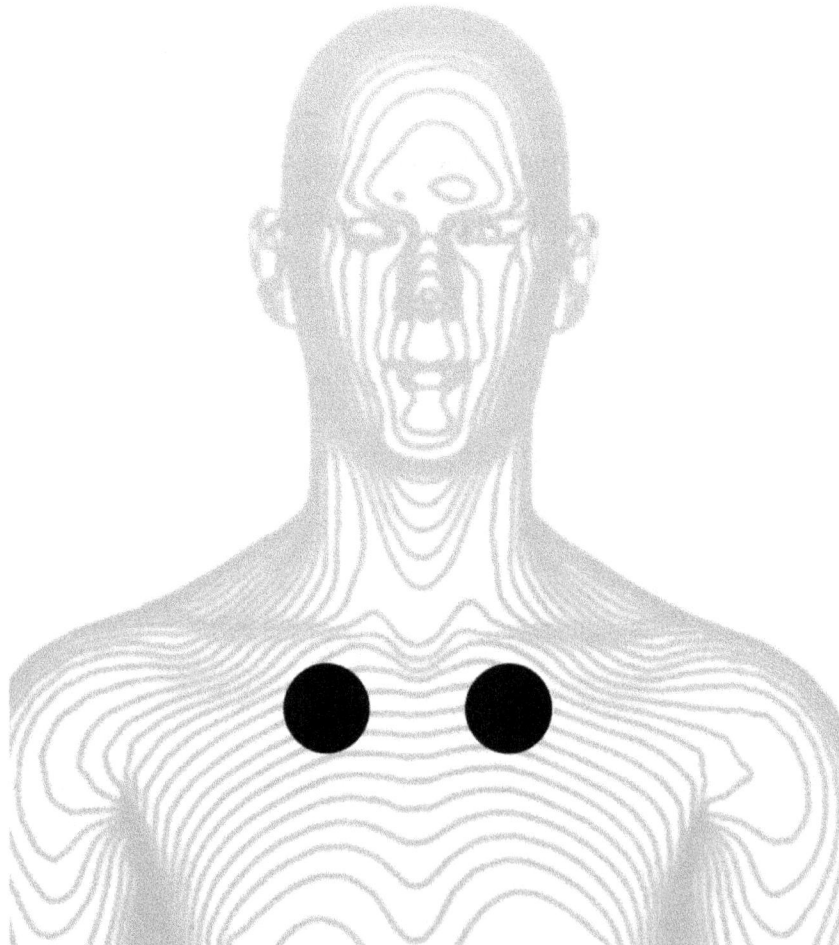

Now that you have cleared your resistance, write out your desired outcome with specific, descriptive words. Experience it as your reality. As you write, imagine the experience in full color and stereo!

Be clear enough if someone were reading this, they would immediately understand. Once you write it out, go back and reread it, fully experiencing every detail. Do this every day for at least 2 weeks.

Tips to Make Visualization Work for You

1. Relax. Give yourself time prior to the visualization to relax. Use the Heart Focused breathing, and unhook from the tension, letting any tightness in your body release and relax.

2. Have a goal. What do you want to achieve with this visualization exercise? It does not have to be a lofty goal; it can be simple. Start with a specific goal.

3. Do not get hung up on how this will happen. I want to share a powerful story of how you can use visualization without trying to figure out the details. If you play golf, you probably know the name Ben Hogan. Early in his golfing career, he suffered a devastating car accident and was told he would never walk again. He told his wife to bring his golf clubs into the hospital room. The physicians were against it because they did not want him to have "false" hope.

Ben had conviction and a strong personality, and his desire won out. His clubs sat in the corner for many months, and as he went through his treatment, he would imagine himself playing the game, swinging the clubs and walking the course. After a year, he did walk again. He went on to win many golf championships.

4. Bring clarity and accuracy to your vision. Make your vision clear and focused. As you imagine, experience this as if it were happening. Visualization engages all the senses.

Some people do not actually "see" images; rather, they feel the experience or think about it. Use all your senses to make this visualization clear and focused. Ben imagined he was golfing and applied his knowledge of the sport to accurately imagine the experience, using all his senses. Musicians apply the detail of their skill and talent to imagine they are playing the piece flawlessly. Use your skill in the area in which you are imagining filling in certain details, allow your body to engage muscle memory when appropriate, and make this visualization very real.

5. Be open. Refrain from using a good or bad type of judgment as you visualize. This is the power behind mindfulness, your mind learns to relax, so you can simply experience the moment without giving it an emotional charge of being good, bad, right, wrong, difficult, easy, perfect or not. If you struggle with believing you will achieve the goal, then back your vision down to something you can experience as real.

6. Stay in the moment. See the vision as happening right now, not next week or next year. Your unconscious mind does not have the dimension of time, and if you see something happening next year, you will always be a year away from your goal.

7. Keep this to you. Do not share your visualization with anyone. This is your goal and you do not want someone else's opinion.

A Simple Exercise in Visualization

As a child, you used your imagination easily. You were not filled with doubt about being "realistic" or worried about being playful, you simply used your imagination to relieve stress and learn.

This is a simple exercise using the basic technique of visualization.

1. Think about something you want. Keep it simple and something you can easily see yourself having. It could be an object, event, or a circumstance.

2. Get comfortable. Make sure you won't be disturbed. Give yourself 15 minutes. Use a timer.

3. Starting from the top of your head, move all the way down your body and relax. Release tension. Count down from 10 to 1 and tell yourself to relax even more as you count down.

4. As you relax, imagine what you want happening exactly as you wish it to be. Feel the experience as if it were happening now. See people coming up to you, your friends smiling, and experience the vivid detail of having what you want.

5. Finish your visualization acknowledging this new reality. You can end with, "and, so it is," or conclude with, "I now have (fill in the blank)."

This is an important part of the visualization. Too often people end up disbelieving the visualization and go back into the fear or doubt mode. This creates only confusion and or ambivalence within you, causing your actions to reflect this.

6. Once you visualize, let it go. Do not think about it. Do this for 15 minutes, every day, for 2 weeks. Journal throughout the process and note any surprises, coincidences, and/or resistance that shows up. Be observant and mindful. Refrain from judging.

Be sure to listen to the audio files in the membership site. The more you learn to relax and allow your mind to wonder (and wander), the easier it is to practice visualization.

FAQ: Frequently Asked Questions About Visualization

Is this still effective if I cannot see images?

Great question. This is one I have heard often. Visualization sounds misleading; this practice is really about *the feeling you have* as you think about (imagine) your desired outcome. The more you practice, the easier it gets.

This doesn't work. I do not see any change.

This is another comment I have heard often. Learning to use your mind deliberately means you have learned to identify and manage your emotions. This means you also are tuned into what you are experiencing during various activities. If you are imagining a desired outcome, but underneath have increased fear or resistance, then, the process is counterproductive.

Practice heart focused breathing and Quick Coherence before you visualize. This opens you up to possibility.

How can I visualize things working out, when everything is a mess?

Learning to deliberately focus your thinking on your desired outcome is the first step to bridging the gap of "doing" the practice of leadership and "being" the leader. It is necessary to keep your eye on the horizon, your desired outcome, while being cognizant of the challenges that lay ahead. This is why mastering your attention is so important. When you are distracted, your burn up precious energy, get exhausted and do not focus.

It is also important to be specific with your visualization. Imagine the details of your desired outcome – then let it go.

Everyday Gratitude & Appreciation (Mood)

Gratitude is a power tool. As you will see in this upcoming module on the coherence building tools, the heart has its own intelligence network which acts as a powerful moderator of the nervous system – when engaged.

The power emotions like gratitude, appreciation and love all serve to reboot the negative consequences of the stress reaction and turn around the hormonal surge of cortisol while regulating the autonomic nervous system and the flight or fight reaction.

The problem is when stress and or pressure is chronic, the ability to feel grateful or pull up some appreciation can be tough. The truth is gratitude is not easy!

Yet, a practice of gratitude and appreciation has the following benefits:

- Makes you happier
- Opens your perspective
- Increases your appeal and influence
- Increases your flexibility and adaptability
- Strengthens your impulse control

As you move through the module on the Power Tools for Resilience you will learn even more of the science behind gratitude and coherence. I hope this will motivate you to build a new habit of gratitude.

Make a list of everything you are grateful for, at this moment. Spend 1 minute and write out everything you can think of:

1.	7.	13.	19.
2.	8.	14.	20.
3.	9.	15.	21.
4.	10	16.	22.
5.	11.	17.	23.
6.	12.	18.	24.

Keep the list on the next page handy and keep adding to the list until you have 100 items.

1.			
2.			
3.			
4.			
5.			
6.			
7.			
8.			
9.			
10.			
11.			
12.			
13.			
14.			
15.			
16.			
17.			
18.			
19.			
20.			
21.			
22.			
23.			
24.			
25.			100.

Here are a few suggestions to bring gratitude and appreciation into your workplace, or your home life.

1. Write 'Thank You' cards.

This is not your typical card. On this card, you want to spell out what impact the person's gesture had in your everyday life and what it meant to you. It is not necessary to write several pages; keep it short, 250-300 word; being specific about how it has impacted you is most important. First, it helps you truly appreciate the gesture and the person who did it. It also coveys to that person the significance of the gesture.

Next, deliver the card in person if possible and have a face to face meeting where you convey your gratitude. Allow the person to share their experience while you actively listen.

This is a powerful experience and will build trust and deepen relationships. As the leader, it will make a big impression on your followers.

2. Keep a Gratitude Jar in the office (or at home).

This is a fun activity for the workplace (and your family). Keep a large, wide mouthed jar (or empty fish bowl) on a desk in a common area. The jar has to have a mouth wide enough to put a well sized hand in and out of it.

GRATITUDE JAR

Next to it put a box with slips of paper, can be white or multi colored to jazz it up. Tape the instructions on the outside of the jar. Every day put in one to three things you are grateful for... encourage everyone to do the same.

Check out the Grati-Slips template on the next page. You also have one to download on the membership site.

Then take out a Grati-slip out every day and reflect on it. Spend time appreciating this; practicing the Heart Lock in. Share your enthusiasm with others.

Gratitude Jar Instructions:

1. Every day, put in one (or more) Grati-slips into the Jar with anything you are grateful for at work. As you write it out, feel the appreciation of this fully, allow the feeling to flood your being and fill the jar.

2. Whenever you start to complain or feel negative, pull out a Grati-slip. Read it. Make a sincere attempt to appreciate what is on the slip. Use the Heart Lock in and let this feeling flood your entire being and fill the jar with your appreciation. Be sure to share with someone, what Grati-Slip you pulled for the day.

Periodically check in with your team and see how this is impacting the workplace. Be sure to review the Bonus Video in the Power Tools module on Group Coherence. It only takes a few people using this tool to change the mood and the culture – but it requires a commitment.

grateful

Grati-Slips

I am grateful for:

I am grateful for:

I am grateful for:

I am grateful for:

I am grateful for:

I am grateful for:

I am grateful for:

I am grateful for:

I am grateful for:

Journal

Write out how this exercise has changed your perspective. What have you noticed in your team, or family, as a result of these gratitude activities.

What gets in the way of your ability to feel grateful? Anger, disappointment, grief? Think about a recent time when you felt stalled. Write it out.

RE-FRAME: BEYOND THE BS AROUND STRESS – YOUR BELIEF SYSTEM!

What you believe drives your behavior. Stress changes your perception and can set up a skewed reaction to what is happening around you.

This next process will reframe "stressed out" reactions and highlight beliefs that may be sabotaging you, giving you the opportunity to do it differently next time.

Use this chart to work through some of the reactions you would like to change. This process works if you work the process. It is well worth it!

Here is an example of starting with a **consequence** and then working back to see what happened.

Activating Event	Beliefs	Consequences	Dispute	Evaluation
		Feel sad, hopeless, hungry. I crave sweets.		

What may be a trigger for these feelings?

Activating Event	Beliefs	Consequences	Dispute	Evaluation
Seeing my co-worker get the promotion I really wanted.		Feel sad, hopeless, hungry. I crave sweets.		

The key aspect of this exercise is to identify the **BS – your belief system responsible for** setting up the chain reaction. Tune into your self-talk.

Activating Event	Beliefs	Consequences	Dispute	Evaluation
Seeing my co-worker get the promotion I really wanted.	Nothing I do is enough. I do not have what it takes.	Feel sad, hopeless, hungry. I crave sweets.		

This part of the exercise is to dispute your beliefs and discard those that are no longer true. Rigorously debate every aspect of your self-talk.

Activating Event	Beliefs	Consequences	Dispute	Evaluation
Seeing my co-worker get the promotion I really wanted.	Nothing I do is enough. I do not have what it takes.	Feel sad, hopeless, hungry. I crave sweets.	1. I am in the MBA program. 2. I am organized and execute, i.e., getting the clinic wait time down. 3. This was not my time.	

Overview

Where is the proof of your belief? List the factual evidence in support of your belief. Emotional storms may capture all your attention and "feel" real. However, feelings are not facts.

List the "logical" explanations to explain the activating event. In the case of this example, seeing the ex and not having a date for the party were paired together as if one caused the other. They are two separate events. Your ex may make you feel like you can never get a date, although they are not really related.

If you were to give advice to someone about this event, what would you tell them? This forces you to be objective.

Have you been in a similar situation before only to find out that it was also a skewed perception? If you are prone to "awfulize," dramatize or "catrastrophize," you may have a pattern that is worth breaking up.

What have you learned from previous situations?

In the final phase of this process, complete the **Evaluation** column and write out how the process of debating and disputing **A**, **B**, **C** shifted your perception and or attitude.

This process is empowering and helps break through the **BS – your belief systems** that have had you stuck or derailed.

Blank ABC Chart

Activating Event	Beliefs	Consequences	Dispute	Evaluation

NOTES

INTRODUCTION TO MINDFULNESS

Start with a decision to be more aware. Then choose specific times during your day when you will focus your attention.

The more often you control your attention, the easier it gets. Here are 3 opportunities to be more mindful:

Routine Activities:

Eating • Brushing your teeth • Shower • Phone calls • Walking to a meeting • Before you enter your home

Body Awareness

Working out • Getting in/ out of the car • Going up and down stairs • Body Scan

Reactions

When you notice an emotional response • After an emotional reaction • With emotions; you may be feeling sad, angry, scared, numb

3 Components of Mindfulness

I find it easier to measure how mindful I am by checking to see if I am engaged in these 3 components.

1. Awareness
2. Objectivity
3. Neutral

The 3 Second Transition: Attention Reboot

Listen to the 2.33 minute audio on the Attention Reboot. Use this technique whenever you are transitioning from work to home, home to work from meeting to office floor, etc.

Suggestions for Using the Attention Reboot:

1. Before you get out of bed - breathe, acknowledge your day, and then get up.
2. Walking into your office. Breathe deliberately and clear your mind, saying to yourself, "I am ready to focus."
3. Before and after any meeting, professional or personal. In your mind, open and close the meeting by using three seconds to: (a) acknowledge what is happening, (b) bring your full attention to the meeting, and (c) bring your full attention back to yourself at the close of the meeting.
4. Before and after every meal. Practicing mindfulness while eating is a great way to eat less and enjoy your food more.
5. Before and after difficult conversations. Keep your attention on what you need to learn about this person or to understand the situation. After the conversation, tune in to yourself and what you need to do to process any raw emotions.
6. Before you walk in your front door at home. Clear your mind and refresh your attention.

FYI: The modules: Coaching, Lifestyle and Movement are not in the manual and only online.

SETTING UP YOUR DAILY PRACTICE

In this section you want to put these tools into practice. Resilience is a set of skills you engage daily to manage your energy and recharge your inner battery, so you can be ready for anything.

Watch the video on the membership site. Follow the instructions to set up your Action Plan.

SUPER TIP

Begin using these tools when you are not necessarily stressed. It makes it easier to use them when you *are* in the throes of the stress reaction!

Here are a few examples of how my clients use these tools:

1. First thing in the am, before getting out of bed: Use Heart Lock in, imagine your day going exactly as planned. And even when things go wrong, see yourself getting through it with ease.

2. On the way to work, practice heart focused breathing, shifting into appreciation as you remember something special about your loved ones.

3. Right before meetings, practice Quick Coherence to reframe any low frequency emotions like annoyance and or frustration. See your meeting as productive.

4. Use Freeze Frame to consider alternatives to situations at work that are not producing the outcomes you want. What might be a more efficient way to handle that situation?

Use the Action Plan on the next page to map out your strategy for using these tools.

Action Plan

When	What: Strategy	Result	Follow up

Journal

What impact will this program have on your life/ your day at work/ your home life? Write it out:

_____

_____

_____

_____

_____

_____

Do you have any resistance about implementing these power tools in your day? What is your self-talk around this? (Once you identify them, be sure to use the energy clearing method on these.)

_____

_____

_____

_____

_____

_____

_____

_____

_____

NOTES

NOTES

NOTES

NOTES

NOTES

NOTES

WORK SMART CLUB

Our membership is designed to fuel amazing career growth and success in the workplace. We know growing, learning and expanding our abilities is part of the human spirit. To support this, we have an amazing library of resources, live and online, to help you achieve your goals.

If you want to more guidance and support to develop your leadership skills, become a great communicator and consistently achieve your goals, consider joining "the Club."

We have toolkits for leadership, productivity, problem solving; hundreds of resources, live support and engaging topics you have access to 24/7.

www.worksmart.club

www.ingramcontent.com/pod-product-compliance
Lightning Source LLC
Chambersburg PA
CBHW081553220326
41598CB00036B/6666